Affirmation

Affirmation

poems

Steve Straight

GRAYSON BOOKS
West Hartford, Connecticut
graysonbooks.com

Affirmation
Copyright © 2022 by Steve Straight
Published by Grayson Books
West Hartford, Connecticut
ISBN: 978-1-7364168-6-0
Library of Congress Control Number: 2021924969

Book Design by Cindy Stewart
Cover Design by Catherine Casalino

For Marian

Acknowledgments

Grateful acknowledgment is made to the editors of the following journals, where several of these poems, some in slightly different form, first appeared.

Amethyst Review: "Drishti"

Common Ground Review: "My Father Enters Another Contest, 1956"

Connecticut River Review: "Janitor," "Old Longtooth," "Varieties of Insect Experience," "Invention"

Connecticut Woodlands: "Intersection"

Eunoia Review: "Traffic Pattern"

Freshwater: "Elixir," "Nowhere, Man," "The Good Ship Steve," "Lachrymose," "Mowing," "The Next Life," "Oh, Possum," "The Sentinel," "Telling the Bees"

Here: "The Future of the World, Part II: Youth," "Tuning," "Biopsy," "Security"

Hartford Courant: "Darner"

Paterson Literary Review: "The Maisie Problem"

Plum Tree Tavern: "Murmuration," "Cruising"

Right Hand Pointing: "Soul"

Rise Up Review: "The Butterfly Effect"

Tar River Poetry: "Casualty," "Seat 1A"

TETYC: "A Murder Question," "Vincent," "Some Assembly Required"

Verse-Virtual: "Imperfection"

Willimantic Chronicle: "Glitter," "Escape Room Pantoum," "Wild Life Trail"

"Cruising" is also included in Grayson Books' *Waking Up to the Earth: Connecticut Poets in a Time of Global Climate Crisis.*

My thanks again to my first mentors, Rennie McQuilkin and Sandy Taylor, and deepest thanks to my wonderful writing group, the Wordsong Poets: Dacia Ball, Lisa Butler, Kate Foran, Vicky Nordlund, John Stanizzi, and Elizabeth Thomas. This book probably wouldn't exist without you.

Contents

3

Some Assembly Required

Hand me the instructions,
the ones with the diagrams
inscribed with numbers and letters,
circles and arrows,
cute silhouettes of "tools you will need,"
the wordless Ikea ones deeply trusting
the spatial intelligence of the customer,
with complex telescoping projections
of bolts passing through washer wood washer nut,
or the ones translated into seventeen languages,
knowing somehow that someone out there
who purchased a thirty-inch Henriksdal bar stool
with back rest can comprehend only Magyar.

Bring on the obscure notes in parentheses
like "do not tighten bolt completely until Step 5,"
or insist on three and a half inch screws throughout the tome
while supplying only three-inchers in the double-zip bag,
or require a slotted head screwdriver when somehow
this afternoon our entire house will cough up only
Phillips head after Phillips head as I walk from room
to room, Styrofoam peanuts clinging to my sweats
and shirtsleeves like pilot fish.

In the crazy schedule I call my life,
give me this afternoon window, a cold beer
and only the responsibility of erecting
this end table, this grill, this pergola
with just the runes of some distant stranger to guide me,
and I am happy to sink into this manual,
this handbook, turning the chaos of the parts
spread before me into their proper congregation.

1

Vincent

The one-eared chipmunk I had fed so many times
last year from my hand, so close I could study
the tumid wound where his left ear had been,
the sucking flies stuck to his striped back,
the tiny toenails manicured by rocks,
did not return this year,

and I imagined all the calamities that chipmunk
flesh is heir to: the silent dive of the red-shouldered hawk,
the neighbor's wily calico, the fox whose baby-squeal
electrifies the night, and even plain old age,
which is never far off for a chipmunk.

And I blamed myself for taming him
to the point he trusted this indentation
in the big stone atop the wall,
that despite his palpitating heart he might have
let down his fidgety guard because of our daily routine.

And so now, when he does appear, three weeks late,
ear hole now healed, and clambers over the rocks
and into my hand, all four feet, even pausing
to eat one of the black seeds as I hold him aloft,
what choice do I have but to stop,

breathe deeply in the palm of the present,
to shuck what isn't and savor what is?

A Murder Question

On a frost-covered morning I hear crows
out in the yard somewhere, their raucous caws
complaining about something over and over
in their hoarse, irritating way.

"What is that racket?" asks my wife,
not a fan of sharp sounds.

"Crows," I say, and looking closer,
"about eight of them in the St. Francis garden."

When after half an hour they are still roosting
in the semicircle of lilacs, like angry barristers
bickering over some point of natural law,

I go outside, thinking of what I know
about this unpopular family, the corvidae,
that they are among the smartest of animals,
have at least 250 different calls and rattles,
will defend unrelated crows from hawks,
that they can remember a specific human face
and even hold a grudge against it.

As I get closer the cawing increases, deafening,
but they don't fly off, as if they have some reason
for perching on these specific bushes in the cold

and then right below, hidden among the hyacinths,
I see it, the dead crow, and I realize the caws
are not complaints or arguments but eulogies.

When I lift the crow with my gloved hands
and then dig its grave at the back of the property
the crows gather in the maples nearby,
softly keening now, witnessing my respects.

Oh, Possum

We know them as gray lumps in the road,
with their long rat tails and triangular snouts,
their fate the result of their defense against
oncoming cars, which is to turn and hiss.

But today I find one at the end
of its two-year journey on earth,
which began as a joey no bigger than a raspberry,
now nearly three feet long, nestled and still
amid our lemon thyme,
under the deep blue and green canopy
of the wild indigo.

How often a mysterious creature in nature
sends me to a book or a computer,
as this one does. The only remaining mammal
that waddled past dinosaurs, this cousin
of koala and kangaroo,
night-shift janitor with few peers,
which grooms itself like a cat, consuming
black-legged ticks at five thousand a season.

Nearly immune to rabies, not to mention
the venom of rattlesnakes and cottonmouths,
the possum thrives in our margins
with most of its defenses just bluff
until pushed to its involuntary coma,
leaking foul excretions to ward off harm,
coming to sometimes hours later
with the wink of an ear.

This one is done playing, done working,
having avoided the bobcats, the foxes and owls,
even the three-legged coyote I saw
loping through the back yard just yesterday.
No more carrion, no more spilled seeds,
no more ripe persimmons in autumn.
Just a gentle repose, an ideal death,
a death to be jealous of.

Mowing

"One man in ten thinks it's a privilege
to push his own lawn mower."
—Thornton Wilder, *Our Town*

Marching behind a Briggs & Stratton-powered push mower,
earmuffs muffling the roar and inducing a kind of tunnel,
I notice today's earworm, which could be anything in 4/4 time,
is thankfully a Randy Newman hook
that will follow me for the whole afternoon.

It is a long walk, some nine thousand five hundred steps,
my Fitbit will tell me, in an order so prescribed after
twenty-one years that I can hardly vary it, like
writing the same short story line by line every five or six days.

As all who mow know, the half loops around trees,
the hillsides, the aggressive vines and wild roses at the edge
are the work, eventually yielding to the great back and forth,
two hundred feet south, the two-wheel pivot, then north
the same distance, shaving twenty-two inches of lawn each row,
in either somnambulance or the kinhin of fine observation.

When the grass is tall after a week of rain or vacation
I scour the forest below, worried for the toad leaping for the daylilies
or the garter snake escaping down a chipmunk hole,
all of this traced to the time I hurtled the mower
on the first tall mow of spring, when the deck passed
over a slight depression and revealed below me
a wrack of rabbits, days old, safe only because I set the deck high.

All are welcome in our lawn, the purple veronica spikes
I mow around for three weeks, the rolling spring carpet
of violets and buttercups, even that enemy of many,
the dandelion, sunflower of the turf. In fact, every time I hear

the neighbors' homogenized swaths of green lauded as "perfect"
I wince, cannot imagine purging from either my lawn
or my vocabulary clover and quackgrass, henbit and
mallow, mugwort and dwarf cinquefoil, chickweed
and snowdrops and spotted spurge, not to mention
Johnny jump-up, Jack–in-the-pulpit, and even creeping Charlie.

Varieties of Insect Experience

How tiny the part that pierces the skin—
the capitulum, the proboscis, the stinger—
those syringes that announce the brief encounter,
followed by the itchy bump, or
the focused fire and swelling,
or the painless incision that becomes the bull's-eye rash.

These are chemical reactions as old as time,
induced by the anticoagulant, the venom, the bacterium,
which often begin in quiet places, perhaps tending the herd
in an open field, sitting for a spell on the fallen trunk,
or kneeling to weed the cosmos.

Most of these are brief and come with our territory,
but we know of malaria, dengue, West Nile.
and the stealthy arthritis of the tick.
And so we tend to these with aloe or plantain,
with Benadryl or cortisone, or with weeks
of Doxycycline gathered in its blue and white capsules.

As I take this morning's dose
with my tall glass of spring water,
I think of Ötzi the Iceman, shepherd or hunter
from five thousand years ago, and the disease
we share, an identical tick latching onto him
as it did me, though it wasn't the pathogen that got him,
but an arrow as the snow began to fall.

Intersection

As I cruise down the long hill
in rush-hour traffic,
two lanes of eagerness each way,
I see ahead some object in the road
I will need to avoid,
a truck muffler, perhaps, by its size,
which cars whiz by and around
without slowing down,

but as I come closer I can see
it is a large snapping turtle,
having left its pond, no longer fecund
or starved by a siege of new houses
ringing its shore,
crossing a border into territory
it does not understand,
at the mercy of power,
its mud-covered carapace
now a useless shelter.

In a better world
strangers would slow and then stop,
backing up traffic both ways
despite the clueless
horns of entitlement
until this wizened being
older than the dinosaurs
could plow ahead,
one stiff step at a time,
this immigrant, this Other,

the bravest among us
getting out of our lives
to lend a hand.

Darner

Morning opens through the fog on the lake
and the three-note wood flute call of the loon
carries through the mist, which makes it easier
to stay in the lapping water present,
hearing some truck in the distance hauling
the past to the future, and as the sun starts
to burn a blue hole from the sky to the water
I return to the puddle of my thoughts.

Then, checking the temp on an outside thermometer,
I see through the glass that trapped in the fabric
of a giant web glistening with dew is a three-inch
dragonfly, what I later will determine is a female
green darner, still as death and covered in silk.

I step outside to study it closer, for once at rest,
its bright green thorax and long brown abdomen
with black line running down the top
and clear wings tinged with amber, a sign of age.

Then I am surprised to see it twitch, and I realize
its thousands of honeycomb lenses in each globular eye
can see me, the mosaic that I am. It twitches again,
and without much hope I grab two small sticks
and try to remove it from its grave.

I set it on the picnic table, and it doesn't look good:
one wing is folded over itself, and it spasms again,
helpless. Then it settles down, and when I pull
the silk off, it straightens its wing, apparently okay.
Next is the goo around the abdomen, so sticky
and strong. When that is gone, it still doesn't fly,
and when I remove my progressive lenses, I see

the tiny legs are still caught. Needing a finer
instrument, I find a piece of pine straw
to hook the silk and extract it speck by
speck from femur, tibia, tarsus until all is clean.

There will come a time, if it doesn't make it back
to Mexico, when the darner is taken from above
by some quick kestrel or below by a bass,
but as it skitters off toward the lake again, I say
to myself, Not today, at least. Not today.

Elixir

Among the things
I would like to bottle,
today, when my friend
Jenny and I
are catching up
between classes
at the high school,
and she notices a black ant
on the yellow tile floor
circumambulating
our tiny island of connection,
and she worries for it
so close to our shifting feet,
and then we return
to our happy chattering,
but periodically she
looks down again,
checking on its progress,
or lack thereof, weaving
between us and then
wandering off and returning,
still worried,
as if this ant matters to her
like one of her students
or even her son,
a little creature dependent
on the rest of us to be caring
and aware,
and I just want that ant
to walk around us forever.

Mikehenge

As I set Mikey's plate down on the kitchen floor
at 6:01 p.m. on July 25th, lo and behold
his sacred ceramic circle is bathed in sunlight

and while I'm not sure about his belief system
he bows to eat the Wellness Chicken and Herring Pâté
as if in prayer.

Of course as a cat he could find his food
in the dark, but surely this shaft of gold
has layers of illumination.

It's a month and change since the holy solstice
but it is the Feast of Saint James,
and on a Sunday, no less

and while this isn't Chichen Itza
or the Great Pyramid of Giza
or even Chaco Canyon

when he rises to circle the plate
in clockwise rumination
and then bends to his task again

I can't help noticing how his four legs
capture the light, and like stone columns
cast shadows dependent on this day and time

and a hush seems to fall over the kitchen.

Old Longtooth

for the Hill-Stead Museum, Farmington, Connecticut

During a drought in 1913 the Italian workmen,
struggling to dig a water trench on the grounds
of the great estate, kept stubbing their shovels
on thick roots of something well below
the waterlogged turf, until one of them
stopped and called out, "Non radice, ossa, ossa!"

And sure enough, as they felt their way
with their fingers now, down through the sticky clay,
they did find bones, heavy and ancient,
what the professor called in from Yale
would confirm was *Mammut americanum*,
the American mastodon.

It's not hard to imagine this stocky elephant of old
standing in the late Pleistocene winter,
his shaggy brown coat dusted with snow
as the flexible trunk grabs twigs and
branches from the lark, spruce, and pine
in the Hill-Stead hills fifteen thousand years ago
as the glaciers retreat to the north.

There are no buildings, of course, no buildings at all,
and the very occasional neighbors are the dire wolf,
the short-faced bear, a beaver of three hundred pounds,
or the giant ground sloth lumbering by in the forest.

Nine feet at the shoulder, with curved tusks just as long,
he was a solitary being, browsing his fill
a full-time job at a weight of five tons,
cracking off limbs with his tusks
and grinding them down with his nipple-shaped molars.

At death there was "no sign of foul play,"
as the professor said, no proof of Clovis hunters
taking him down, just a few thousand years
from extinction, anyway, having roamed the earth
for a million. Tuberculosis may have claimed him.

If one were still around, as Jefferson had hoped,
no doubt it would be chained somewhere, trotted out
for show under threat of the bullhook, a spectacle
in a world that seems to feed on celebrity.

Whatever drew you to this swampy depression,
moss or pine cones or just a drink of pure water,
I for one am glad you are not here today
to see this circus, this three-ring earth.

Wildlife Trail

Perhaps it was naïve of me
to turn down Apple Orchard Lane
past the new McMansions
with their pairs of spindly new maples
and expect to find at the end of the street
an apple orchard.

I should have known
there are no longer foxes on Fox Run,
no blueberry bushes sagging with fruit
on Blueberry Circle, and of course
no old farm on Old Farm Road,
no farm at all.

Eventually it dawned on me
that the one thing I would not see
on Pheasant Way, Quail Run, and Woodcock Lane
is a pheasant or a quail or a woodcock,
all having long ago departed
for some small remaining rectangle of space.

Named for what they replace, or drive out,
like the generic doom of Wild Life Trail,
they might as well be called Dodo Avenue, or
Passenger Pigeon Place, or Woolly Mammoth Terrace.

Why not some honest names
for these mausoleum streets:
Overconsumption Highway,
maybe, or Entitlement Circle,
or perhaps just the Boulevard of Greed.

Telling the Bees

*Traditionally if there is a death in the family
or some other sad event, bees in hives
are informed by their keepers, in part to keep
something worse from happening.*

In my vented full-body suit with helmet and veil,
gaiters covering my ankles, long goatskin gloves,
I approach the hive.

Some say this should be done at midnight
but I have come in early morning,
a light dew on the grass and mist rising
off the long river in the valley below.

I drape the hive with black crepe,
then knock gently, once,
to tell them I have come.
I listen to their electric buzz.

How to tell them how much trouble
we are in, how close we are to ruin,
how very much we need their help.

In a little rhyme, perhaps, as is tradition:

> *The earth still spins, little bees,*
> *but we dread what lies ahead.*
> *Save yourselves, and save us, please,*
> *before our global hive is dead.*

Bees know the world is round,
what zero is, how to dance
the angle of the sun even when

it's on the other side of the world,
how to make food that lasts
for thousands of years.

I, on the other hand, don't know anything.
Exhausted by the smoke of doubt and fear
I long instead to be stung again
by wonder, by joy.

Rap for Castor

for Ben Goldfarb, author of Eager: The Surprising, Secret Life of Beavers and Why They Matter

This poem must be read aloud, with energy.

You got problems out west, you're runnin' out of water
Temperatures risin' and the world's gettin' hotter
Tryin' to mitigate floods and stop runaway fires
You got water in quantity but not where you want it to be

You gave us no respect, so what did you expect?
You thought a buck-toothed rodent would be better as a hat
So you trapped us and snapped us until you're all that
Too stupid to see that you were fracking up your habitat

You exceeded your need until greed was your creed
Had a shizzle vision of your mission, to speed
a landscape raping you should have been arresting
Now I guess your destiny is manifesting

They call me The Beaver
No, not the one by Ward Cleaver
Castor canadensis
Genus? I'd say genius

We shaped the contents of the continents
Masters of geology, ecology, hydrology, topology
Our diligence, intelligence, experience, and innate sense
could handle any consequence

Now you need us more than ever, brother
If you want to last forever and recover
Looks like you could use a furry god mother

Give you pristine streams, replenish all your aquifers
A salmon run replacin' all the damage done
Another keystone species where there isn't one
Just keep in mind the beaver battle cry:
Wetlands Are the Best Lands, and that's no lie

With us it's just pond to wetland to meadow to forest
And day or night, oh, the concatenatin' chorus
So we'll find a dam spot just where you needed one
Now leave it to the beavers, man: We'll get the job done

2

Inheritance

after two photographs

One fourth of my genome sits on a tractor
with a kind of fez on his head,
head cocked, with half a grin.
He is 91, about to start the day's chores.
I know he had trouble seeing the camera
and couldn't have heard the "cheese" clearly.
But there's no escaping the twinkle,
no escaping the strong, liver spotted hands
that signify a life of milking cows
and clearing fields of stones
and making do.

Once he came to our house,
and my father warned him about petting the cat.
Still, he couldn't resist, and at the first stroke
the cat striped his hand.
I remember the look on his face,
neither shocked nor annoyed.
The same half grin as on the tractor:
Life is interesting. It has been worth it
to live this long. Even my own blood intrigues me.

Another fourth of my genome sits on a wooden bench
between his house and the lake in Pennsylvania.
He is 66, wearing only tropical-print swim trunks,
reading a book called *Dreams.*
With his round belly and bald head
and big, toothy smile,
he is the Buddha on vacation.

Twenty-five years earlier, in seminary,
blowing perhaps too hard on the coals of inquiry,

stressed by money woes,
with three daughters at home
and headmaster of a failing school,
he snapped into a manic state
and came to believe he was Jesus.
It took the fire hose of early shock therapy
to reduce him to the mellow soul I knew.

In the photograph he is beaming. At me.
The look on his face says, Yes, there is all that,
or was. But now there is this.
Now there is you.

Base Eight

It's just another sleepy afternoon
in eighth grade math class when Mr. Caouette,
with his plaid jacket, bow tie, and silver flattop,
turns to us and with a wink says,
"I think it's time you learned
there's no good reason we count to ten,
instead of, say, eight." The chatter ceases,
and we 12- and 13-year-olds shift in our seats.

He chalks the numbers 1 through 9 on the board,
says, "This is called base ten, the system we use.
The Hindus invented it, in India, and then the Arabs
picked it up in trade, and Fibonacci brought it to Europe."
I'm pretty sure I couldn't spell Fibonacci.
He spreads his fingers wide for us,
as if hands have just been invented.
He wags one digit on each hand, says,
"They call this nature's abacus, and
it seems obvious to us why we use ten,
but no one really knows."

Then at the board he erases 8 and 9,
and after 7 he writes 10: "Base eight," he says,
"it could have easily been like this."
He asks us to "think in base eight," and we begin
by bumping our ages up two years—cool—
and then computing the year, now 2460 A.D.

Someone in the back is skeptical,
gripping the desk of certainty tightly,
and Mr. Caouette asks, "Why do we measure
in twelves? Inches in a foot, three twelves in a yard?
What about time? Seconds in a minute,

minutes in an hour? That's Babylonian, base sixty."

That evening I can't wait to tell my father.
A systems analyst in the early days of computers,
he knows all about it, of course, and casually adds,
"With computers, you can store and manipulate
all of knowledge with just a binary system, base two."

Suddenly so much of life is arbitrary, even math.
I begin to wonder what if anything can be counted on.
Prodded by my father, I find myself
in the folds of the *Encyclopedia Britannica*,
swiveling slowly in the black vinyl chair
by the fire, staring at a photograph of a giant
sunflower head in the entry for Fibonacci,
following its perfect, dizzying spirals of seeds
that curl into infinity.

My Father Enters Another Contest, 1956

Twenty-five words or less but they mean less.
Let me swing open our old Frigidaire here and
plop my chair down rightchear in the opening,
let that cool air wash over me like a bath.
Like a bath. Hmm. *A cool bath for your food.*
For your milk. *A cold bath for your beer.*
It's good and hot outside so this feels like
some kind of miracle. That's not bad—
Feels like a miracle. I can remember hauling ice
on the farm when I was a kid, you know, packing
it in hay in the barn—so that cold bottle of milk
I'm looking at right now reminds me how easy
it is these days, a brave new world, like
instant winter. *The miracle of instant winter.*
The instant winter miracle. Winter in the middle
of summer.

If this main compartment's winter, the freezer
box must be the Artic. *The Arctic for your ice.*
Ice straight from the Pole. A little too obscure.
They don't want obscure. When I won that radio,
they didn't want Marconi, they wanted
A box seat at a private symphony.
Too bad I can't use Freeze your ass at the Hotel
Buster—remember that joke?—Oh hell,
take a streetcar! Wait a second—Frigidaire.
Frigid air. Right smack in front of me
all this time. That's good, that's good.

Let's open the door and close it a few times,
let the cool waves come out. What about the light?
Even in the dead of night you can fumble
your way down the hall, find the handle,

and you're all set. *The loyal light. The light*
that waits for you. The guiding light. See,
that's good. That's why it stuck.

Let's try imagining that new GE rightchear.
Probably got umpteen gizmos, lazy Susan
jobbies on the shelves, dedicated egg bins.
GE: the wizards of widgets. A spot for every
chicken. GE makes you say Gee whiz.
The power to control the weather. GE stays cool
in desert heat. A little Canada right in your kitchen.

Sometimes even when you've got it, you don't
know it. That's life. Maybe I should just go out
and think about it while I cut the grass. *Toro:*
a bull for your lawn. Makes tall grass say olé.
No, wait, hang-gon, hang-gon—
At GE, we keep your life cool.

Janitor

Each night you haul your tall
cardboard barrel with the steel rim
down the long hall from office
to office, emptying the baskets
into it one after the other.
That's why at the end
of the first month that muscle
at the base of your thumb
is a swollen knot of granite.

After the workers in ties
or skirts have left for home
you move down the row
of toilets in the tall marble bathrooms
scrubbing each clean with stiff
bristles, then sink by sink
with chlorine powder
and a damp grey rag.
To this day in a public restroom
you are likely to cup
your fingers and splash water
around the bowl after
you've washed your hands.

Eventually it doesn't matter
to you that none of it will be clean
for long, and sometimes
an accountant working late
comes in the second after it shines.
You have no trouble now
putting the first dirty spoon
into an empty dishwasher.

Once a week you polish
the forty-foot brass rail,
rubbing the Noxon with your rag
in small, muscular circles,
removing the patina
six inches at a time,
leaning in close enough
to smell the ammonia, then
letting it dry to white clouds
you slough off with clean cotton.
You know full well
even in this golden moment
that life begins to oxidize
right behind you.

Security

Pratt & Whitney Machine Tool

Three thirty p.m. and I step onto New Park Avenue
at a break in the factory-shift traffic of 1974
and walk to a spot between the double yellow lines,
the zipper of this four-lane road meant to be two,
dressed in my polyester Wackenhut uniform
with black clip-on tie, tuxedo stripes down the sides
of the legs, a police hat with a silver badge
that means nothing, another pinned to my shirt
hidden under the bright orange vest three sizes too big,
then raise one orange glove that stinks of the sweat
of dozens of guards who've passed through this job,
this spot, this hat, attempting to convince the drivers
rushing home or to work to stop for this
nickel-above-minimum sham of a cop so I can release
the stream of workers pouring out of the lot
at the end of their shift, truck drivers especially
hating me for making them grind through their gears
all over again, more than one after the token blast
of an air horn giving me two or three seconds to duck
under the stiff side mirror as they ignore my glove.

The tool-and-die men don't like to be stopped either,
eager to escape their tedious hours tending the jig borers
and milling machines two stories high reaching
into the dust-speckled light streaming in through
the windows sixty feet up, men with dull eyes and
plugged ears standing by their machines as I walk past
on my clock round, curlicues of steel peeling off the blades
onto the wood-brick floor soaked with decades of oil,
all this explaining the popped trunks I pretend not to see
as I tour the lots on their dinner breaks,
exposing the coolers of Schlitz.

The guards are another story, the weekly parade
of new faces I try to train, all of them at the bottom
like me, a step above unemployment, excepting the gung-ho
wannabes with their police scanners and salutes,
most barely able to sign in the truckers, confounded by
an eighty-key clock round that winds through the plant,
making one quit the job mid-round, the Detex clock and his hat
and tie found later in the maze of the plating rooms,
one kid taking a good long look at me directing rush-hour
traffic before shaking his head and leaving ten minutes into the shift.

This is what it meant to drop out of college back then,
choosing the inside of the factory or the outside,
pushing carriages through the snow at the local grocery,
reaching a paint brush over the gutter at the top
of a wobbly ladder, or hauling bricks or shingles or
lumber or copper pipes to someone with real skills.
So I put in my two years on the second shift
until the darkening afternoon one winter day
when the streets were slicked with ice, and as I held up
my bright orange glove to stop traffic in one direction,
a car trying to obey me went into a skid down
the double yellow line right toward me and
I had no choice but to step back blindly into
the other side of traffic, stepping back into my future.

P. bivitattus

Softened by camaraderie and Molson Goldens
after a night as darts partners,
stranger became acquaintance,
and when at one a.m. the bar closed
and he asked if I'd help him with a favor
for a friend on campus, I said sure.

The favor involved trekking to the biology lab,
a turf as foreign to me as a jungle in southeast Asia,
my only associations dim memories from high school
of Bunsen burners and deep black sinks
and a frog with splayed legs that my X-Acto blade
hovered over for a good long time.

When we entered the dark lab in the bowels
of the building, he flipped a switch and cockroaches
swarmed toward corners and cracks and under the desk.
I imagined the task some cleaning of cages
or checking of inventory—gerbils, perhaps,
or rabbits, but as we approached the far corner
his face sobered with each step.

He paused before a large glass enclosure,
its top weighted with large stones, and inside
below a branch the largest snake I ever hope to see.
"Burmese python," he said, not taking his eyes off it,
"about eight feet. It's not eating the dead rats."
Sure enough, several rat bodies larger than my hand
littered the cage, the snake showing no interest.
"We'll have to remove them," he said.

The snake perked up as if in response,
uncoiling and coming down stage right,

its tongue testing the new chemicals in the air.
And when my acquaintance announced
that we'd have to take the snake out first,
I wondered if this stranger had ever held
the snake before, or any snake.

I was to learn later that a python has heat sensors
along its jaws but terrible eyesight,
so it easily confuses prey and keeper,
and will strike large animals it could never eat
just in case it can. Adult deer. Alligators.

He removed the rocks and folded back the top,
exposing us to the snake, still flicking its tongue.
And then he reached inside and grabbed it behind the head,
barely holding on, and there was nothing to do
but grab the other end with both hands.

As we lifted the creature out of the cage,
it was instantly clear the snake disapproved,
and as I held the surging river of muscle,
the prehensile strength of a tail the size of my thigh,
I knew that if my partner somehow dropped his share
or if the coil now around his wrist tightened sufficiently,
the snake could easily strike, coil around me, and
had water been nearby, drag me under for good.
The idea of removing the rats while holding
the snake's head with one hand now revealed
as a monstrous joke, we were left holding an alien power,
the history of Asia, perhaps, or the revenge of all
mistreated species, or simply a powerful argument
that I should be doing something more serious
with my life than shooting darts in some bar.

Nowhere, Man

After we turned off Route 7,
I think it was,
and stopped meandering
along the Housatonic,
and took that left by the old mill,
crossed those railroad tracks
and found ourselves in a deep valley
on a narrow road with no turnoffs,
when Siri stopped talking to us
and our phone announced "No Signal,"
we knew we were in the boonies
for sure, that is to say out in the middle
of nowhere, the sticks, past Podunk
and East Overshoe and even East Jebrew,
and judging by the rusting truck
out back of that house down to
its last rows of shingles, its mailbox
stove in, we were in Hicksville, Rubeville,
some jerkwater town without a stop light,
past East Jesus and on the way to Timbuktu,
nearly to Upper Buttcrack, the back side
of beyond, if you know what I mean,
not that we were lost, but let's just say
we were out past the spot
where Christ parked his bicycle.

Invention

After seeing a ranking of the greatest inventions
of all time, all day I see inventions: on my desk alone,
the *ballpoint pen*, the *paper clip*, the *stapler*,
the *rubber band*, all from the 19th century;
the *timepiece*, five hundred years old; and
of course, *paper*, when Cai Lun, in the Han Dynasty,
mixed fishnets, old rags, and mulberry.

The list of course holds the big ones
in high esteem: the *lever*, the *wheel*, the *compass*,
the *abacus*, and perhaps surprisingly at #47,
the *nail*. The list makers are careful to distinguish
between the mere discovery of fire, that blaze
in the forest that crept closer, and the *control of fire*.

It is a day I take less than usual for granted
as I steer my *automobile* down the *macadam*
and cross the *railroad* tracks before waiting
at the *stop sign*, which came originally
in a variety of colors. I begin to appreciate
things not on the list, as when I pause to admire
the *interlocking facial tissue* that releases one at a time.

Most of the inventors are lost in the fog
of progress, of course, but there is *Morse code*,
the *saxophone*, the *Zamboni*. The lineage
of some inventions is striking, Edison's
light bulb traced back to Egyptians dipping
their hands in the Nile and being shocked by electric fish.

I now appreciate the fine line between invention
and discovery—George De Mestral returning
from a hike in the Alps with his dog, picking

burdock burrs from clothes and fur, then studying
one under a *microscope*. He chose a portmanteau
of *velours* and *crochet*, but it could have been *mestral*.

As I squat before my wood stove,
I realize I am mighty pleased with my own
contribution, this short stick I discovered
on the ground and fashioned into a smooth poker
with a *hacksaw* and *sandpaper*. I will call it
a *straight* and use it now to poke this fire
into submission.

The Good Ship Steve

First I learn that deep within the forest
of hair follicles on my eyelid—
and yours, most likely, if you are old enough—
lives a community of tiny mites,
Demodex folliculorum, apparently farming
the coarse terrain of my skin
and taking nightly strolls across my face
to visit with friends, perhaps in my nose.

Then I read that these wee creatures,
small as they are, have their own bacteria,
no doubt doting on them in some fashion,
and my sense of scale starts to get a little tipsy.

Soon I am drunk on the idea
that several hundred *species* of microbes,
to the tune of a hundred trillion bacteria
form a thriving commonwealth on my skin,
in my mouth, and of course in the dominion of my gut.
I could borrow a microscope to confirm
all this, but I think this time
I will take the scientists at their word.

Mostly freeloaders, commensals, or favor traders,
some with a new generation every twenty minutes,
much of the time these guys keep the pathogens out,
for which I am grateful. I must apologize
for the occasional antibiotic typhoon.

At ten resident microbes for every single cell
of my own, I gradually become uncertain
who or what I am, a commander, with duties,
merely a protectorate with a striped flag,

or am I just a slow freighter ferrying them
everywhere, just as Hannibal did
over the Alps, and Cook around the globe,
not to mention Armstrong on the moon,
himself a little mite wriggling on a skin of dust.

Selfie

In the top of the first inning
the man behind the backstop,
by his bright red team jersey probably
a StubHub chump paying top dollar
to sit so close to the field, just this once,
has realized that each time the pitcher
comes to rest in his motion,
fingers feeling for the stitches,
that he is momentarily in the frame of the shot
from the centerfield camera four hundred feet away,
and so now he is waving to that camera
and to all of us at home ensconced in our couches
and recliners, our formerly empty lives now complete.

He is close enough in the third row
to see the flat-screen monitors embedded in the wall
for the well-heeled denizens to check replays,
and he begins to watch himself waving on the screen,
waving to himself it seems, and waving back.

In the first inning he waves on every pitch,
trying to extend his Warhol window,
keeping his eyes on the monitor to make sure.
By the second inning his achievement
has worn a little thin, so now he is on the phone
to tell a friend to watch him wave,
and he waves harder, but after a little while
you can tell that thrill is gone for both of them,
and by the fourth inning it's call after call—
"Guess where I am, Fred," "Guess where I am, Wanda"—
whomever he can reach who can be coaxed
to a television to watch him, well, wave.

After he's run out of friends, co-workers, and
distant cousins, he keeps it up, perhaps
feeling obliged now to all those he called
in case they are still watching,
until it's the queen's wave, a stiff wrist
atop a swiveling forearm, to conserve his strength.

In the seventh inning it strikes him
to preserve this bit of personal triumph
and so he lifts his phone in front of his face
to capture his spot in the stands, then
turns around to snap his view of the field,
out where some people seem to be playing
some sort of game.

The Sentinel

The knitted brow gives him away.
While others at the meeting choose their diversions—
doodling, working a crossword, starting a new poem—
he takes voluminous notes on nothing,
combing his colleagues' words for discrepancies,
transgressions, for perceived agendas.

Committee reports? Administrative hoops?
Endless lists of new and old business? All grist
for this miller, picking nits out of the previous minutes,
grinding minutiae into fine powder,
then snorting it to maintain his focus.

As we move into the second hour of tedium
and attention wanders for most to picking up the kids,
or the first glass of wine, he's deep in the bunker now,
squinting into the periscope, wary of motions,
amendments from the floor, shooting down
any attempts to circumvent The Rules.

When nearly all is said and done,
when those who have lives will return to them,
when we're down to announcements
and goodbyes and all can sense the ending,
don't even think about asking if there are questions:
His hand is already up.

Imperfection

What a perfectly gorgeous day here
at the lake cottage we're renting in Maine,
although the dock could be just a bit longer.

I'm not sure why there's only one Adirondack chair
down by the lake. And I wish that loon
would come a little closer to shore.

They promised a teakettle and there isn't one.
We'll have to buy a bulb to get any light in the fridge.
You'd think every cottage would have a cocktail shaker.

The downstairs is pretty musty, if you want to know the truth,
even though we're not using any of its four beds.
Is that a faint septic smell from next door?

Oh well. I guess I might as well swim out to the float
before we have gin and tonics on the deck
as the lobsters come to a boil.

Still, those kids in the water two docks down
have no idea how their voices carry,
no idea at all.

Biopsy

Before the oncologist calls
with the results, and we hear
whether my wife will have to endure
another two years of surgery, radiation,
and chemo sickness, her hair
falling out in clumps,
white cell count dropping
precipitously—or worse,

or not

we pretend to vacation by the lake,
and I notice the lone maple
turning orange and red prematurely,
the dark clot of cloud moving over us,
and down in the middle of the lake,
someone's unmoored raft
drifting with the current.

After the call and the tears
and the hugs and more tears
only then do I see the pair of loons
circling each other across the lake,
the newly opened waterlilies
by the shore, sunlight replacing shade
as the cloud moves north

and when my wife flings
the ice cubes from her drink
over her shoulder into the lake,
the tiny rings spread out
in perfect concentricity

until eventually the surface
returns to glass.

3

Seat 1A

on the Beechcraft 1900D
from Toronto to Hartford
is a serious seat, I realize
when the tall, thin copilot suddenly leans
down from the low cabin ceiling
into my face just before takeoff

and over the fever of sound
from the warming twin turboprops
asks if I am prepared
in the event of an emergency
to save all eighteen passengers,
nine on each side,
by pushing this red button
and releasing this rounded lever up—
or was it down?

He monkeys his way into his seat up front
and begins to flip indecipherable switches
almost absentmindedly,
the roar shut out by his huge headphones,
but I am so sobered by my charge
that I see I am also what stands
between the exposed, now deaf pilots
and some crazy lurching down the aisle.
My wife in 1B has a bad elbow
and may not be much help.

But then I think,
Aren't we all in Seat 1A now,
having received our instructions,
acknowledged the stakes,

sized up our fellow passengers
and vowed in any event
to save all we can.

Cruising

for Tony Hoagland

We're standing on the top deck of the *Apocalypse*,
Prestige Level, its wastewater fouling the sea in our wake
as off in the distance the moonlit iceberg of awareness
pokes through the surface of our comprehension,
though ninety percent of it lurks below.

Ten percent is about all we can take
yet still not enough to change our ways,
not enough to link the polar bear stranded on its tiny floe
to the steak, medium-rare, on our bone china plate,

the zooplankton ingesting the molecules of plastic bag
we used yesterday to cart home the romaine lettuce
grown in the sunny concentration camp
of the Salinas Valley,

lobsters scuttling north to cooler water
as longhorned ticks bushwhack their way
into new territory, the heroes of some other story,
while we buy clothing treated with permethrin
or spray our kids with DEET
to think ourselves safe from the viruses.

Down south, the mangroves know all this,
their roots knitted together in a fiber-optic system,
collecting and sharing data from their leaves,
doing their best to excrete excess salt or store it in their tissues,
stabilizing shorelines and taming tsunamis
until it's all too much, even for experts.

Can you hear the musicians?

The ones asked to soothe all the passengers?
Years from now they will find one of the rosewood violins,
surprisingly pristine, and exhibit it in the Museum of Civilization.

Entropy

for Christine Blasey Ford

As a hurricane of images rushes by,
coal ash toxins spilling into rivers
of hog waste lagoons plunging toward the sea,
carrying the flotsam of a civilization,
history and science and rational thought
scraped from town after town in its path
toward an ending beginning to come into focus,
gulls shrieking under a blazing sun
as a stiff breeze comes in off the ocean,
plugs of oil sludge bobbing in the waves,

suited officials in a distant room
tighten the knots of their prejudices,
lean forward on their chins to feign listening
as the senator from South Carolina
gavels the hearing open in the stifling room
with three resounding thunks
as flashbulbs pop.

The witness sits at the oak table,
demure in a dark green suit,
fingers folded patiently.
"Miss—"
"It's Ms."
And there is the smirk,
subtle yet arrogant.
"Very well, Mizz, uh, Gaia.
Now could you describe
your claim that you were violated?"

Escape Room Pantoum

This map of the Arctic might be a clue.
Remember: solutions can be large or small.
Is it warm in here, or is it just me?
That clock is fast, if I'm not mistaken.

Remember: solutions can be large or small.
Right now we're trapped inside our own notions.
That clock is moving faster than it was.
I wonder what the rubber boots are for.

Right now we're trapped inside our old notions.
If we don't solve it, will we get a new room?
Now water seeps in; that explains the boots.
Things don't seem connected but they really are.

If we don't solve it, will we get a new room?
Is it wicked hot in here, or is it me?
Things don't seem connected, but alas they are.
This map of the Arctic just has to be a clue.

Casualty

The rabid ones, yes, the beheaders
and torturers, the suicide bombers
strolling casually into the market at noon,

and probably the commanders and generals
doling out such orders, snug in their bunkers
with the charts and maps of abstraction,

and the soldiers and rebels and insurgents,
I suppose, though many are conscripted
or their families threatened or so poor
that fighting seems like an option.

But today, reading news of the latest war,
out of duty more than curiosity, I am
stopped by the report of the donkey

strapped with explosives and sent
toward the enemy, carrying its load
as it does every day, and some line
seems to have been crossed.

I am not forgetting Armenia or Nanking or
Dresden or Cambodia or Rwanda or Darfur
in a list too long for a poem.

But somehow on this fragile morning
I can't stop seeing the rebel with his sash
of bullets prodding the farmer with his rifle

to turn and look at his animals, the tall ears
of his donkeys, the tufts backlit by the rising sun,

the coarse mane and soft fur and dark eyes,
ordering the farmer—"Choose the one."

Lachrymose

Summer, 2020

Every day now begins with tears.
As soon as I am upright,
a tear forms in my left eye
and will keep doing so the rest of the day
no matter how many times I dab it
with my shirtsleeve.

They tell me it's actually "dry eyes," somehow,
as if denying the liquid before their eyes,
that my tears may be of poor quality
and my lacrimal gland is overcompensating.

But these are the same eyes
that see the news each morning,
that read of peaceful protestors
sprayed nightly with federal tear gas,
that watch as leaders turn a blind eye,
that witness the eye of our national storm.

And since I cannot touch my face
the few times I am out and about,
for fear of contamination,
the tears trickle down for all to see,
and no amount of cotton or tissue
can stanch how I feel as with my good eye
I see this vale of tears now in sharp relief.

Throwing It In

The woman up ahead in the left-turn lane
is never going to put her signal on.
The driver in front of me is not putting down
his cell phone to think about driving.
The woman in the car next to me
is not about to stop berating her kids,
who stare at their hands and try to swallow.

All our food is not going to come from local farms,
the animals snorting and cackling
their lives away until the humane slaughter,
the vegetables fertilized with composted manure,
pesticide signs on front lawns gone the way of the dodo.

Congress is not going to take money from billionaires
to feed hungry children, to get every veteran
shelter and peace, to right four hundred years
of racial inequity and shame.

The meek shall not inherit the earth,
at least not while it's still capable
of making a profit, not while the earth can still breathe.
And let's just say the peaceful reign
of all beings on Earth
is just not happening any time soon.

And so perhaps it is finally time
I relaxed my shoulders
from their permanent shoulds,
exhaled the breath I have been holding in
for fifty years or so,
gave my adrenal gland the rest of the year off.

I have hoped so long and so hard
that people of all generations
would act from the deepest truths
and not from prejudices chewed like cud
I have been slow
to acknowledge that my desires
for the world really have no effect.
I can hardly get the cat to come
sit in my lap, for God's sake, can't
get water to boil in a pot before its time.
My attentiveness has no mass.

So here, world, is my official towel:
I'm throwing it in.
I'm shucking the yoke
of eternal optimism once and for all,
accepting the tea of reality,
and I can feel my frame,
hunched all this time
from the exhaustion of yearning,
begin to release already.

Don't think I won't vote,
or read the newspaper,
or give up teaching my students
not to be fooled. It is time, though,
for folks younger than I
to take up the reins of expectation,
to pull them taut in one hand
while the other raises overhead
the whip of confidence,
the whip of will.

The Maisie Problem

I was out on my daily walk when I came upon Todd,
our neighbor in the gray colonial, with Maisie,
his shaggy, excitable mutt, who had a green
tennis ball in her mouth, just in case.

Maisie came bounding up to me,
prancing at my feet as usual, then
bucked my hand with her head for pets,
but Todd seemed a little sheepish.

"Got a question for you, neighbor."
"Shoot," I said.
"We're wondering if you might take care of Maisie."
"Sure," I said. "When?"
"I'm not exactly certain, but soon."
"Going somewhere?"
He pointed to the sky and smiled.
"Cool. Disney? Europe?"
"No, um, The Rapture."
Maisie dropped the ball at my feet.

"We were at our church last Sunday,
you know, the one on Avery Street,
and our pastor said we'd better get ready,
that the Rapture Index was at 189."
"That's high?" He nodded. "Imminent.

"Problem was at dinner that evening,
our Annie, she's nine, asked if Maisie
would be raptured with us. My wife and I
looked at each other, but we had to tell her No.

"Well, Annie gave the dog a scrap of fat

from the table and said if Maisie couldn't go
then she wasn't either." He shook his head
in disbelief. "I tried to explain dominion
to her, but she wouldn't have it. She said
if we could find a good caretaker, maybe
she'd consider going."

"How'd you think of me?"
"We've seen you out in the yard
on Sunday mornings when we drive
to church, so we figured, well,
he's probably not a true believer."
Maisie looked up at me through her shag.

"What makes it so imminent?" I asked him.
"You know, look at the world: All the
earthquakes, that eruption in Hawaii,
famine, holy wars, all the signs, and then,
of course, Jerusalem," holding up his hands
as if to say it should be obvious. "And the president,
doing God's work even though he may not know it.

"I won't be able to text you, I don't think,
so maybe if you just check the news for,
you know, thousands of Christians
suddenly gone missing, caught up and all,
then you'll know to see about the dog."
He looked down at Maisie, relaxed now.

"Of course, if you change your mind,
you know—about Jesus—just let me know."
Maisie looked up at me, then at Todd,
then down, at her bright green ball.
She had plenty of fetch left in her.

Ouija

In a bag by the back door
my wife has left an old Ouija board,
the "mystifying oracle" in its original box,
lid tied shut with ancient string, knotted,
and I know without asking
that she is weighing the karmic consequences:
Will the spirits be upset
to find their telegraph in the trash?

The questions begin innocently
at the seventh-grade sleepover,
the bedroom lit by a single candle,
the parents fast asleep down the hall,
one girl asking "Which boy likes me?"
as the plastic, heart-shaped planchette
slides inexorably to the letter J,
then the letter O, at some point
causing a friend to squeal, "You're moving it!"
"I am not."

Past midnight the questions turn
to the occult: "Is evil near us now?"
"Which of our friends will die first?"
accompanied by the slight scratching sound
as those beyond dole out their messages
letter by slow letter.

The jury is still out on whether
the spirits mean well or ill, and
if the act of asking is tinged with the demonic,
but even if the answers are flawed or problematic
it is clear by our long history of consultation,
of the shifting charts of the stars,

or creases in the palms,
or coins or yarrow stalks
tossed to form a hexagram,
not to mention dominoes or dice,
runes or special cards,
scrying with a crystal ball, and
even the entrails of sacrificed animals

that we want to ask, want to establish
a connection between the unchanging eternal
and our tiny finite flesh and bones,
want to believe the nexus could just be
a flat piece of plywood sold by the Hasbro company
and stamped with the alphabet,
numbers zero through nine,
the moon and sun, and the word *Goodbye*.

I ask my wife if we should consult the board
to determine its fate, but she will have none of it,
opting for Goodwill, so someone else
can wrestle with their desire and their skepticism
even if both halves of the name *Ouija* say Yes.

Drishti

Standing on my left leg, knee slightly bent,
my right knee lifted high in the warm air
of this room at the community center,
both arms raised and wrists limp,
I hear our yoga teacher remind us all of *drishti:*
Find a spot on the floor in front of you,
a fleck on the tile, a bit of pattern in someone's
towel. Now soften your gaze so that you are
looking but not looking.

The hard stare seems to be the way to see
the world these days, reading five newspapers
a day and hopping from website to website
waiting for the alchemy of reporting
to reveal the golden nugget that will
bring down these evil clowns,

but as my shaky crane pose shows,
that way of looking, of being,
opens the window for the winged monkeys
of attachment, snatching attention
and carrying it off in their sharp claws.

Perhaps it is time to find
the unmoving point in all of this,
reduce the existential wobble,
to imagine the horizon in front of us
no matter where we are, find
the Steadicam of the mind that stills us
when all about is shifting, tectonic,

or even, now,
to gaze at a candle in the dark

with eyes open until they water,
bathing and cleansing the vision
with the tears of renewal:
one flame, one heart.

The Next Life

Sanibel Island, Florida

Standing on this Florida beach
as the day approaches dusk
I think of my brother-in-law's desire
to return in the next life as a pelican,
and now five glide by, inches above the water,
wings perfectly still under the waning sun
and one peels off lazily and climbs
to dive for menhaden.

It's hard not to mock those devotees
of past-life regression who emerge
from their sessions of hypnosis
convinced they were once a queen of Egypt
or dallied at the court of Catherine the Great,
not peasants slogging through the muck
to their thatched huts and gruel.

Pressed for an answer to this eternal question,
after our attempts to ask it in different ways,
a Zen master I once knew eventually sighed
and said, "What if it is more like a cue ball
hitting a ten ball, say, passing energy
from one to the other?" and then he smiled.

Still, after visiting the site of a shell mound
I am drawn to the humility of the Calusa,
who peopled this region for at least 12,000 years
and who believed we reincarnated into
ever-*lower* forms until we disappeared—
and now I feel all the kings and conquistadors,
panthers and peasants, turtles and

pinfish and clams, their former souls
squishing between my toes.

Soul

Soul is like an idiot on the town green,
dressed in odd clothes that make people keep
their distance, can float a spider on a head
of beer and read the future, slippery though it is.
A promiscuous thing, flirting with a succession
of lives, soul takes the long, long view,
a tack that compresses moments
into diamonds. Linked without thinking
to the *anima mundi* and all its brethren,
soul stays attached to us by a thin silk thread,
feeling the vibration of our mortality.
At night, soul walks back through the town green,
slapping the side of its head, laughing
at a joke we're not sure we want to hear.

The Butterfly Effect

*"A ten-year-old boy with obsessive-compulsive
disorder thought the 9/11 terrorist attacks
were his fault because he did not step on a
particular white mark on the road that day."*

The link between the white mark and the horror
seems slim, yes, but the OCD in me,
though mild by comparison, is sympathetic.

And probably there is someone in a small, drab room
arranging pennies in strict rows
to stave off world financial collapse,

someone replacing all the washers
in all the faucets in the house again to, you know,
keep the oceans from rising farther,

someone washing their hands raw
to cleanse the world of hate and prejudice,
of tribalism and inequality.

Look, I know what you're thinking,
that these are all just remote rosaries
for people unsure of God,
who haven't been granted the wisdom
to know the things they cannot change.

But how else do we stop the random,
delinquent gene that switches on the cancer,
the virus that turns the body against itself,
and especially a vile microbe
that gets elected president?

Each thing that's happened

could have been prevented,
can never be prevented,
says the Zen master,

but if intercession works,
as science begrudgingly concedes,
who is to say what little bit may help?

So I finger the beads, one at a time,
beads of bone, beads of wood,
working out my place, my part.

Traffic Pattern

Amalfi coast, Italy

The Strada Statale 163, road of switch
backs and hair
pin turns needed to nego
tiate the jagged silhou
ette of cliffs and fj
ords,

the Via Smeraldo, built by the Romans,
who perhaps imagined a future civilization
where the brake is your horn, where
narrow corniche roads are shrunk further
by rows of parked Smart cars and Fiats and
even vegetable trucks hugging
the stone walls, plus pedestrians
two and three abreast on the wrong side of the street

not to mention the crazy *motorini*
who invent their own lanes in the middle,
zipping nimbly around any and all vehicles
even on curves, even in tunnels, even
on curves in tunnels, then calmly
tuck themselves back into traffic,

where drivers routinely cut people off
and are cut off themselves, all without
incident or harsh words or fingers
perhaps because the day is so beautiful
and the smell of ripe lemons and apricots
fills the air high above the Tyrrhenian Sea

and yet here comes our city bus in one direction

and a large Mercedes paneled truck in the other
and everything comes to a stop.

In a real clog, as when a side street empties
into the fray and snarls everything,
bus and truck drivers shut off their engines
and climb down to sort it out,
backing up streams of tourists in rental cars,
the *amatori*, and although marked by the occasional *buffo!*
this is also sport and not argument,

but today the bus driver and paneled truck driver
merely inch their large rectangles toward each other,
toward a kind of sacred spot only they can sense,
bougainvillea scraping through the side windows,
the drivers' dark eyes shifting from mirror to mirror
as they gradually align their ships,
perfectly parallel ten centimeters apart for ten slow meters,
and we all return to our zigzag lives.

The Future of the World, Part 2: Youth

On the way in from the parking lot
I see a student with a big Bruins shirt over shorts
on a cold day in March, headphones, backpack
slung over one shoulder, gangling toward class.
Almost past a trash can whose plastic lid
with swinging door has blown off in the stiff wind.
To my astonishment he stops, and then replaces it,
fitting the lid securely all around the circumference.

As I approach the main entrance I hang back
and study the behavior of the students:
six in a row hold the door for the next person,
who lets it close behind her just as another
gets to it; he holds it for the next, who then
totally ignores the heavyset woman
carrying two bags, a pocketbook, and holding
the hand of a toddler. I race for the door,
she thanks me heartily, and I hold it
for the next student, who says nothing.

Like the binary foretelling of daisy petals
in my youth, I think:

There is hope. There is no hope.
There is hope. There is no hope.

Intro to Lit, opening day prompt:
"Talk about yourself and reading,
perhaps a favorite book."
Three of twenty-five begin,
the ones who've brought books
they're reading: a Stephen King,
a sci-fi series I don't know,

and one—God bless him—
Zen and the Art of Motorcycle Maintenance.
Then about six in, a young man, with tie,
admits, "I don't really like to read."
As if a giant permission switch were flipped,
hands shoot up around the room.
"Yeah, I hate reading." "Oh, me too."
Too many nods to count.

There is hope. There is no hope.
There is hope. There is no hope.

After a morning when I discover most of my students
don't know how many senators New York has,
can't tell me one thing about Gandhi, cannot name
the date of the Declaration of Independence—
"1876?" "1920s?" and one belligerent shrug,
between classes I see a young woman
swinging her red-tipped cane down the hall
approach a giant clot of young students
she may not sense how dense, lost in their cells
or shouting random things to each other—
but all at once they part and give her a wide berth.
All eyes follow her down the hall
and I hear someone say, hushed:
"She's memorized the school, man."

These days, *pianissimo*, under my breath,
I can't stop counting my rosary:
There is hope. There is no hope.
There is hope. There is no hope.
There is hope…

Tuning

Soft mannered, polite, he removes his shoes
at the door and pads in his stocking feet
between the Hazleton grand and the Baldwin upright,
striking the A above middle C on each piano.

Both are slightly flat in the dry air of winter,
and he begins with the Hazleton,
thumping the A440 fork on his knee
and then stroking the key whose tone he will reconcile.

It is slow work, sounding the A steadily
as he turns his hammer in minute increments
until the tone is true, then aligning the intervals
among all the keys in equal temperament,
working his way up the keyboard for the next hour.

I am most content to listen one room removed
so that his healing work is clear but softened,
and unlike my musician wife who makes excuses
to leave the house for this, I feel myself each time
fall into trance, as if I were being tuned.

It is a languid pleasure, hearing the relationship
between discordant beings resolved two notes at a time
until order is restored, all tension removed,
and in time the whole house is in tune,
if not the world outside.

Glitter

April, 2020

Slowed to a crawl, isolated from each other,
turned inside ourselves by this invisible glitter
that travels as a fine mist
and clings to everything, or might,

we are all poets now,
savoring the garden soil between our fingers,
astonished at the sprout of a pea
unfurling from the dark,

aware now of each flash of goldfinch
to and from the feeder, the confetti
of white petals snowing from the pear tree,
across the street a shimmering vernal brook,

while far above us the sky heals itself
right before our eyes.

Murmuration

*"A failure to realize that a property is emergent,
or supervenient, leads to the fallacy of division."*
—Issam Sinjab, astrophysicist

Two women in an old canoe
at late-winter dusk on the River Shannon,
one filming, one paddling as gradually
a matrix of dark spots roils on the horizon:
birds, starlings, by the thousands, forming
and reforming clusters of swarming shapes,
funnels and ribbons and hourglasses
folding over each other and then swirling high
in the air, still cohesive and without turbulence,
as the women laugh in awe.

It is their simultaneity that dazzles,
how a giant game of Telephone transports
the message to turn or dive with electric speed,
and as the physicists say, without the signal
degrading, in scale-free correlation,
each shift a critical transition
when they move as an intelligent cloud.

What roils them in the gloaming
as they prepare to roost, it turns out,
is usually a peregrine falcon,
the fastest animal on earth coming in low
at the edge and then shooting upward,
its blue-grey back and black head blurred
as the flock reacts as one.

These days we too sense something
coming in fast and low, coming for us
as we turn and turn in our widening gyre

of discord and tumult and strife,
and now the choice is ours.
There is safety in numbers, I suppose—
it might take her but not me—
but will we hear instead what is emerging,
or can, the greater song that says
we are but cells of a giant heart
ready to pump new blood.

Affirmation

"We need to be fanatical in our optimism."
—*Steve Almond*

*Note: This is intended as an oral poem. The speaker
should improvise specific details of setting and actions.*

*We live in a beautiful, harmonious world
      without war, or pestilence, or famine.*

It was a single voice in the room,
      almost lost in the shifting of people
      in their metal chairs.

*We live in a beautiful, harmonious world
      without war, or pestilence, or famine.*

Most of the people listening thought he was crazy.
The most cynical frowned and began to close
      their briefcases and zip their coats.

*We live in a beautiful, harmonious world
      without war, or pestilence, or famine,*

he said again, without flinching. In fact,
he smiled. He noticed that someone else smiled, too.
As he saw the look on that person's face,
he knew the next time he said it
      he might not say it alone.

*We live in a beautiful, harmonious world
      without war, or pestilence, or famine.*

People still shook their heads
        at such a quavering chorus.
That will never be, they thought.
He's a dreamer,
        and the time for dreams is gone.
A few, however, wondered what it would be like
        to say it out loud just once.
The next time it comes around
        maybe I'll whisper, some thought,
        forming the first "w" between their lips,
        and here it came.

We live in a beautiful, harmonious world
        without war, or pestilence, or famine.

Others were adamant, and crossed
        their arms or looked at their phones.
That is not the answer, they thought.
What could a simple sentence possibly do,
        no matter how many people said it?
Gandhi is dead, and so is Martin Luther King:
Who are you against cheeks puffed from beatings,
        against fingers that no heat will uncramp,
        against a small cough like a second hand,
        against hunger and apathy and despair?
But his faith came from his bones, and he smiled again.

Now he implored them:
        Please, would everyone try it this time,
        just to see how it feels? What could it hurt?
        Please, everyone, join us.

We live in a beautiful, harmonious world
        without war, or pestilence, or famine.

That was good. That showed some power, he said.
I don't mean to try your patience,
I won't be up here much longer,
but how about one more time, much louder.
        Ready?

We live in a beautiful, harmonious world
        without war, or pestilence, or famine.

Thank you. Now let's make it happen.

About the Author

Steve Straight was professor of English and director of the poetry program at Manchester Community College. His full-length collections include *The Almanac* (Curbstone/Northwestern University Press, 2012) and *The Water Carrier* (Curbstone, 2002), which was a finalist for the Connecticut Book Award in Poetry. For many years Straight directed the Connecticut Poetry Circuit, and for many summers he directed the Seminar Series for the Sunken Garden Poetry Festival. He has given workshops on writing and teaching throughout the eastern United States. In 1998 he was named a Distinguished Advocate for the Arts by the Connecticut Commission on the Arts. He lives in South Windsor with his wife, Marian Maccarone, soprano and voice teacher.